THE POCKET Weed

Published in 2025
by Gemini Gift Books
Part of Gemini Books Group
Based in Woodbridge and London

Marine House, Tide Mill Way,
Woodbridge, Suffolk IP12 1AP
United Kingdom
www.geminibooks.com

Part of the Gemini Pockets series

Cover illustration: Shutterstock Ltd/CNuisin

ISBN 978-1-80247-283-7

A CIP catalogue record for this book is available from the British Library.
Disclaimer: The information in this book is solely for informational purposes only. The manufacture, possession and distribution of marijuana (also known as weed) for any purpose is illegal and against the law in the United Kingdom and throughout many jurisdictions throughout the world. The Publisher does not encourage or advocate acting in any way that violates any local, regional or international applicable laws or regulations. Portions of this book describe activities that may be hazardous and/or illegal. The information presented in this book does not constitute a recommendation or endorsement of any company or any product. The reader is solely responsible for following all laws, regulations and codes of practice relating to the use of marijuana and or any type of illegal drugs. Gemini Adult Books Limited, part of Gemini Books Group Limited, makes no representations or warranties of any kind, express or implied, with respect to the accuracy, completeness, suitability or currency of the contents of this book and specifically disclaims to the extent permitted by law, any implied warranties of merchantability or fitness for a particular purpose and any injury, illness, damage, death, liability or loss incurred, directly or indirectly, from the use or application of any of the information contained in this book.

Manufacturer's EU Representative: Eurolink Compliance Limited, 25 Herbert Place, Dublin, D02 AY86, Republic of Ireland. admin@eurolink-europe.ie

Printed in Poland
10 9 8 7 6 5 4 3 2 1

Image credits: Shutterstock: Single leaf / CNuisin; Cannabis plants / Cyro Henrique; 8, 28, 70, 76, 86, 89, 92, 123 / Pavel Klubovich; 16, 26, 37, 38, 44, 48, 51, 57, 62, 63, 64, 74, 75, 100, 103, 118 / redgreystock.

THE
POCKET
Weed
G:

Contents

Welcome to the Weed Revolution!

The esteemed 1960s artist Bob Dylan once famously sang that "the times they are a changin'", and he could not have been more right. Especially about weed. Which he loved.

For most of the 20th century, the world was at war with weed – it was widely blamed for social decay and creating generations of hippie stoner layabouts.

There's no doubt that the plant's reputation, stature and cultural importance has evolved dramatically, as has our understanding and appreciation of it.

The Pocket Weed is a celebration of wacky-backy (as your parents still call it) and its renaissance from everyone's favourite drag to simply being dope.

Enjoy!

Chapter One

Herb Your Enthusiasm

Tunes & Tokes

Listening to music while enjoying a spliff is one of life's greatest pleasures. *Rolling Stone* magazine agrees.

In 2020, at the height of the COVID-19 pandemic, it devised a list of the 40 greatest albums to listen to while stoned. It does not disappoint.

1. *Axis: Bold as Love* – Jimi Hendrix
2. *Dummy* – Portishead
3. *The Dark Side of the Moon* – Pink Floyd
4. *Paul's Boutique* – Beastie Boys
5. *Rubber Soul* – Beatles
6. *Kid A* – Radiohead
7. *Live/Dead* – Grateful Dead
8. *Merriweather Post Pavilion* – Animal Collective
9. *African Herbsman* – Bob Marley
10. *Mellow Gold* – Beck

The pandemic is responsible for accelerating our love of weed.

According to data reported by the *Guardian* in 2022, legal marijuana sales increased by 120 per cent in 2020 and Americans bought $18 billion (£15 billion) worth of cannabis, $7 billion (£5.8 billion) more compared with 2019.

Hollyweed

In 1976, Danny Finegood achieved infamy when he became the first person to change the Hollywood sign in Los Angeles to read "Hollyweed", a prank that became global headline news. According to CBS News at the time, Finegood's wife, Bonnie, said: "It wasn't a prank, it was a message. He was having fun making a large statement to the world."

The prank has been repeated several times since. On New Year's Day 2017, Zachary Fernandez repeated the stunt using white curtains he'd brought from home. He was arrested for trespassing.

"I smoke an early morning joint regularly."

KEITH RICHARDS,
THE DAILY TELEGRAPH, 27 JULY 2015

"This is like if that Blue Oyster shit met that Afghan Kush I had – and they had a baby. And then, meanwhile, that crazy Northern Light stuff I had and the Super Red Espresso Snowflake met and had a baby. And by some miracle, those two babies met and fucked – this would be the shit that they birthed."

SAUL (JAMES FRANCO),
PINEAPPLE EXPRESS, 2008

Pineapple Express

Hollywood's greatest love letter to weed is perhaps the 2008 cult classic *Pineapple Express*, starring Seth Rogen and James Franco. The film is named after the *Cannabis sativa* strain of the same name, which has a pineapple-esque fragrance. In the movie, Dale (Rogen) compares its scent to "God's vagina".

The plot is thick with smoke: stoner Dale and his dealer Saul go on the run after Dale witnesses a murder involving a corrupt cop and a drug lord. They accidentally drop a joint containing a rare weed strain called Pineapple Express leading the criminals to hunt them down, triggering a chain of events as dope as the strain itself.

Pro Tip #1

Next time you're on a roll, don't use a cardboard filter or cigarette filter. Use a piece of uncooked fusilli pasta instead. *Seriously.*

Due to the twisted shape of the fusilli, the airflow is consistent and even and the pasta itself imparts a smooth starchiness to your smoke.

“The illegality of cannabis is outrageous, an impediment to full utilization of a drug which helps produce the serenity and insight, sensitivity and fellowship so desperately needed in this increasingly mad and dangerous world.”

CARL SAGAN, IN AN ESSAY UNDER THE PSEUDONYM 'MR X' IN *MARIHUANA RECONSIDERED* BY LESTER GRINSPOON, 1971

“Why write I still all one, ever the same,

And keep invention in a noted weed,

That every word doth almost tell my name,

Showing their birth and where they did proceed?”

WILLIAM SHAKESPEARE,
FROM ‘SONNET 76,’ 1609

Shakespeare Stoned

A little-known secret is that the world's greatest playwright William Shakespeare could have written many of his masterpieces while high on weed.

According to scientists who carried out excavations at his Stratford-Upon-Avon estate in 2001, they reportedly found 24 pipes in Shakespeare's garden, eight of which contained traces of cannabis.

A half-century before Shakespeare's time, King Henry VIII demanded many English farmers to grow vast amounts of hemp for his Navy, so it's not unthinkable that William Shakespeare sparked up from time to time.

"The first time I got high off marijuana was in the seventies, with one of my uncles. My uncle lit one up, and I hit that motherfucker. I was eight or nine years old."

SNOOP DOGG,
ESQUIRE, JULY 2008

The Chronic

In 1992, iconic rap producer Dr Dre – the hitmaker behind Snoop Dogg, NWA and Eminem – released his debut hip-hop album, *The Chronic*. Its success transformed the US musical landscape.

The word "chronic", now the de facto term to describe premium weed, was first coined by the rapper Snoop Dogg in 1991 when he misheard the term "hydroponic"* as "hydrochronic" when he was smoking a particularly potent weed strain. Snoop shortened it to "chronic" and you know the rest.

*Hydroponic weed is a cultivating technique that doesn't use soil, preferring a nutrient-rich water solution instead. The potency of hydroponic weed is much greater due to an increased THC content.

4:20

In the last 20 years or so, 4:20 (pronounced "four-twenty") has become the preeminent cannabis culture slang for smoking weed, especially in the USA.

This is because in 1971, five high school students from San Rafael High School, California, coined the term "4:20" as they met at 4.20 p.m. to go on a quest to search for an abandoned cannabis crop, based on a treasure map made by an anonymous grower.

After several failed attempts to find the crop, the phrase 4:20 eventually evolved into a code for going to hang out by a local statue to smoke weed. Now, it's used to refer to consuming cannabis – but as it's part of the vernacular, it doesn't make such a good code word...

Today, 20 April – the 20th day of the fourth month – is celebrated as International Cannabis Day.

Did You Know...

The first ever online purchase was a bag of weed.

In 1972, 25 years before the advent of Amazon and eBay, students at Stanford University, California, used the university's ARPAnet – a precursor to today's Internet – to buy an "undetermined amount of marijuana" from students at Massachusetts Institute of Technology (MIT), the other side of the country.

“Of course I know how to roll a joint.”

MARTHA STEWART, INTERVIEW AT 92ND STREET Y, JUNE 2013

Cannabis Kings (& Queens)

Like whisky, tequila, coffee, wine and champagne, weed has become big (legit) business, especially for celebs looking to cash in on cannabis' renaissance.

Today, scores of celebrities own legal marijuana brands that sell both THC and CBD products ranging from oils to beverages, edibles to pre-rolled joints, including Snoop Dogg, Whoopi Goldberg, Woody Harrelson, Jay-Z, Kourtney Kardashian, John Legend, Bob Marley (estate), Gwyneth Paltrow, Mike Tyson, Willie Nelson and Seth Rogen.

Rhianna's Roll-up

The most unbelievably cool pop culture moment of all time has to be when pop singer Rihanna rolled a fat blunt on top of her bodyguard's bald head (while sitting on his shoulders!) as he casually meandered through a packed crowd at the Coachella festival in California in 2012. Iconic.

Bye-Bye Bongs?

With the rise of legal cannabis, bongs and marijuana-based paraphernalia are slowly decreasing in popularity, it seems. For decades, of course, bongs were a massive feature of cannabis culture in both movies and student bedrooms.

The first bong, it is believed, dates back to around 2,500 years ago with evidence of bong parts found at a Scythian (*see page 117*) grave in what is now part of Russia. The word "bong" comes from the Thai word *baung*, a cylinder of bamboo used as a tobacco smoking pipe.

Icons of Weed #1

Snoop Dogg

Perhaps the most famous weed smoker in the world – currently, at least – is American rapper Snoop Dogg.

He once notoriously claimed that he smokes up to 80 joints a day, according to *GQ* in 2023. He's also not shy about praising his beloved herb, either...

“Weed makes you aware of your surroundings. It makes you watch your back. But, most importantly, when dudes smoke together it spreads peace.”

SNOOP DOGG, *HIGH TIMES,* OCTOBER 2020

Names of Strains

There are too many cannabis strains to name them all in this pocket book, but suffice to say you should try out the types below – and pay close attention to differences in the smell and psychoactive effects. Some listed are classics, and some are new cultivars. Which ones have you tried?

1. Acapulco Gold
2. Afghan Kush
3. Animal Cookies
4. Bash
5. Bubba Kush
6. Chernobyl
7. Fruity Pebbles
8. Gelato
9. Gorilla Glue
10. Grandaddy Purp
11. Green Crack
12. Haze
13. KGB, AKA Killer Green Bud
14. Maui Wowie
15. Northern Lights
16. OG Kush
17. Pineapple Express
18. Pink Panther
19. Purple Haze
20. Runtz
21. Sinsemilla
22. Skywalker
23. Super Silver Haze
24. Tahoe
25. Wedding Cake
26. White Widow

Did You Know...

Different strains of weed are created by cannabis breeders who cross-fertilize a mother plant with another type of cannabis strain, selecting certain genetic characteristics of both plants, such as smell, taste or potency. The offspring of that plant will be an entirely new, and purer, strain.

The Chernobyl Strain

In April 1986, the Chernobyl Nuclear Power Plant in Northern Ukraine exploded. It remains the worst nuclear disaster in history. Afterwards, scientists observed that the radiation had contaminated the surrounding soil, ensuring no life would grow here again.

To reverse this, Ukraine's Institute of Bast Crops planted *Cannabis sativa* around the abandoned site. The plant, with its roots 8 feet (2.5 metres) long and short growing season, is unparalleled in its ability to absorb nutrients (or contaminants) from soil. The last time they checked, in 2019, the cannabis had significantly "reduced radionuclide soil toxicity", according to BBC reporting.

To honour this achievement, there are strains of weed named Chernobyl, which are famed for their sweet pungency.

“What is the different types of hash out there? We all know that it’s called the bionic, the bomb, the puff, the blow, the black, the herb, the sensie, the chronic, the sweet Mary Jane, the shit, Ganja, split, reefa, the bad, the buddha, the home grown, the ill, the maui-maui, the method, pot, lethal turbo, tie, shake, skunk, stress, whacky, weed, glaze, the boot, dime bag, Scooby Doo, bob, bogey, back yard boogie. But what is the other terms for it?”

ALI G, INTERVIEWING A DEA AGENT,
DA ALI G SHOW, 2003

“Marijuana, if used in moderation, plus loud, usually low-class music, makes stress and boredom infinitely more bearable.”

KURT VONNEGUT, *FATES WORSE THAN DEATH*, 1991

"It'd be a lot cooler if you did."

Now a much-loved meme, this phrase began life in coming-of-age cult classic *Dazed and Confused* (1993), when high school stoner David (played by Matthew McConaughey) asks character Mitch Kramer if he has a joint. Mitch replies "No", leading David to speak this now-legendary line.

How Do You Get High?

Getting high is actually a lot more complicated for your body than it sounds. Let's break it down into five simple steps, just in case you're reading this while buzzed.

1. When cannabis is smoked, its active ingredient, THC, is filtered from the lungs into the bloodstream.

2. The bloodstream carries the THC chemical to organs throughout the body, including the brain.

3. In the brain, the THC chemical connects to specific cannabinoid receptors on nerve cells that naturally have the ability to detect these specific chemicals.

4. The THC over-activates – stimulates – the nerve cells causing them to behave differently.

5. Users feel "high" – an intoxicating mix of deep relaxation and/or energy often accompanied by hunger, memory loss and the giggles.

Stoner Movies

Films about heroin or cocaine addiction tend to be dark, twisted and serious. Stoner movies, however, tend to be more comedic. Here's our cherry-picked Top 10 stoner comedies, in no particular order.

1. *Half Baked* (1998)
2. *Friday* (1995)
3. *Dazed and Confused* (1993)
4. *Harold & Kumar Get the Munchies* (2004)
5. *Pineapple Express* (2008)
6. *Dude, Where's My Car?* (2000)
7. *The Big Lebowski* (1998)
8. *Jay and Silent Bob Strike Back* (2001)
9. *Your Highness* (2011)
10. *Smiley Face* (2007)

Pro Tip #2

When one side of a joint burns faster than the other, this is called canoeing.

To prevent it, simply rotate your joint in your fingers as you light the tip it to ensure all the paper is evenly lit.

A Bit of Biology

Like all plants, cannabis comes in several species. The two main species from which cannabis strains are derived are: *Cannabis sativa* and *Cannabis indica*, or a hybrid of both.

Sativa, from the Latin word *sativa*, meaning "cultivated", has a higher THC content and lower CBD content than *C. indica*. Users perceive it makes them more energized and euphoric. This strain originated in Central Asia. It gets you *high*.

C. indica has a higher CBD content and lower THC than *C. sativa*. Users perceive it to make them feel more chill and relaxed. This strain originated from Southern Asia and the Middle East, in particular the Hindu Kush mountain range in Central Asia and India – hence the name. It gets you *stoned*.

“That is not a drug. It’s a leaf.”

ARNOLD SCHWARZENEGGER,
PUMPING IRON DOCUMENTARY, 1977

Good Work!

According to *New Scientist*, the potency of marijuana has increased 60 per cent since the 1960s.

Between the 1960s and 1990s, the THC content in marijuana was less than 4 per cent.

Today, it can be as high as 28 per cent, if not higher, due to cannabis breeders cross-fertilizing more potent strains.

It's Time

Prestigious American magazine *Time* first reported on "the weed" in 1943. The article read:

"To its users, the drug has many names – many of them evasive. Marijuana may be called muggles, mooter, Mary Warner, Mary Jane, Indian hay, loco weed, love weed, bambalacha, mohasky, mu, moocah, grass, tea or blue sage. Cigarets [sic] made from it are killers, goof-butts, joy-smokes, giggle-smokes or reefers. The word marijuana is of Mexican origin and means 'the weed that intoxicates'. It is made from the Indian hemp plant, a spreading green bush resembling sumac. Known to the pharmacopoeia as *Cannabis sativa*, it is a source of important paint ingredients and rope fiber as well as narcotics. It can be grown easily almost anywhere, hence tends to be inexpensive, as drugs go."

"It really puzzles me to see marijuana connected with narcotics... dope and all that crap. It's a thousand times better than whiskey – it's an assistant – a friend."

LOUIS ARMSTRONG, IN A LETTER HE WROTE TO PRESIDENT DWIGHT D. EISENHOWER, 1954

Louis was the original "viper", the term used for 1950s musicians who popularized weed in the burgeoning jazz club scene.

Chapter Two

Four Twenty

Seal of Approval

President Obama was once known as "the Interceptor", according to *Vice* magazine (2014). His love of weed was so strong he would intercept joints as they were being passed around.

Obama even thanked his weed dealer in his school yearbook. "Thanks to: Tut [his grandmother], Gramps, Choom Gang [his marijuana-smoking friends], and Ray [his dealer] for all the good times."

“When I was a kid, I inhaled frequently. That was the point.”

BARACK OBAMA, *THE NEW YORKER*, 2006

28 August 1964

The day music changed.

The Beatles were staying at New York's Delmonico Hotel while on a leg of their US tour. Here, they received a visit from singer Bob Dylan who brought with him his personal weed stash. As they smoked together, Dylan was surprised to learn that the group did not smoke cannabis.

"I don't remember much [of] what we talked about," John Lennon was quoted in the Beatles autobiography *Anthology* (2012). "We were smoking dope, drinking wine and generally being rock'n'rollers and having a laugh, you know, and surrealism. It was party time."

After this, the Beatles smoked on a daily basis and their music was never the same again.

Weed Units

Gram, eighth, quarter, ounce – there are as many ways to weigh cannabis as they are to consume it. At legal dispensaries around the world, the dried and cured cannabis flower is measured and sold by weight. The standard unit of measurement for cannabis is the gram.

1 eighth = ⅛ oz = 3.5 g (*approx. 7 joints*)

1 quarter = ¼ oz = 7 g

1 half = ½ oz = 14 g

1 ounce = 28 g

1 pound = 453 g (*approx. 900 joints!*)

Free Plants?

In June 2022, Thailand became the first Asian nation to legalize medicinal cannabis, labelling it a "controlled herb".

They launched this new relaxation of law with a controversial policy: authorities gave away one million free medicinal cannabis plants. Naturally, within two years the Thai weed market has become dangerously unregulated.

Pro Tip #3

When rolling the perfect joint, be careful not to over-twist the filled paper at the ends.

Doing so will result in too tight a joint, which then won't smoke properly.

One of the most common names for marijuana worldwide is pot.

The origin of this slang comes from the Mexican thirst-quencher *potación de guaya*. This drink is an intoxicating fusion of wine steeped in *Cannabis sativa* flowers and was enjoyed by Mexican soldiers and labourers for its thrilling effects.

What's in a Name?

When it comes to understanding the difference between cannabis and marijuana (or weed) there are three essential facts to remember. (There are more than 540 chemicals in a cannabis plant, but these are the only ones you really need to know about.)

1. Cannabis refers to *all* the products derived from the *Cannabis sativa* plant, including marijuana, hashish and CBD products.

2. Marijuana *only* refers to the part of the cannabis plant – the buds, or flower – that has psychoactive effects – THC.

3. Tetrahydrocannabinol (THC) and Cannabidiol (CBD) do different things: THC gets you high; CBD doesn't.

“I used to smoke marijuana. But I’ll tell you something: I would only smoke it in the late evening. Oh, occasionally the early evening, but usually the late evening – or the mid-evening. Just the early evening, mid-evening and late evening. Occasionally, early afternoon, early mid-afternoon, or perhaps the late-mid-afternoon. Oh, sometimes the early-mid-late-early morning... But never at dusk.”

STEVE MARTIN, *STEVE MARTIN: A WILD AND CRAZY GUY*, 1977

Weed Revolution

With the 21st century weed revolution currently in motion, there has been a rapid rise in legal cannabis dispensaries in the United States.

As of October 2024, there are 15,000! A quarter of these dispensaries (around 3,000) are located in California. Half of these are in Los Angeles, the city with the most amount of legal weed dispensaries anywhere in the world.

A Sign of the Times

When Colorado became the first US state to legalize recreational marijuana in 2012, the Colorado Department of Transportation noticed that every time they replaced the highway mile marker 420* it kept disappearing again within 24 hours.

They soon realized that the signs were being stolen, presumably by stoners.

To combat the theft, they began replacing the 420 signs with mile markers that read 419.99. These too are regularly stolen.

*"4:20" was the clandestine code, predominant in US high schools, for smoking weed behind the bike sheds (*see page 22*).

Cat Piss

From Skunk* to Diesel, really good weed should have a potent pungency. Perhaps the most famous *sativa* strain is Cat Piss, renowned not only for its energizing, euphoric effects, but also its sweet, pine-tree scent, with a splash of ammonia. It reminds users of, well, that horrible cat piss smell.

*Skunk smells like a skunk's spray, but that's a good thing – it means it's super potent!

“They lie about marijuana. They tell you pot-smoking makes you unmotivated. Lie! When you’re high, you can do everything you normally do just as well – you just realize that it’s not worth the fucking effort. There is a difference.”

BILL HICKS, *BILL HICKS: REVELATIONS*, 1993

Beautiful Evolution

The *Cannabis sativa* plant evolved into its current good-time species about 27.8 million years ago, splitting from its closest genetic relative, *Humulus lupulus*, the plant that gives us hops for beer.

Up until around 4,000 years ago, *Cannabis sativa* was indigenous to Central Asia, on the eastern Tibetan Plateau, when it began to be cultivated and used by Chinese farmers for oil and for fibre to make rope, clothing and paper.

“They’ve outlawed the No. 1 vegetable on the planet.”

TIMOTHY LEARY, FROM A LECTURE AT THE UNIVERSITY OF CALIFORNIA, BERKELEY, 1991

According to University of Pennsylvania research from 2018, the average American joint contains 0.32 grams of weed.

This works out to be ten tokes of a standard-sized joint, or five bong hits.

La Cucaracha

Made famous in the times of revolutionary Pancho Villa, in the early 1900s, "La Cucaracha" is a Latin American folk song that Villa's soldiers sang during the Mexican Revolution, a time when many Mexicans emigrated to America – and took with them a lot of cannabis seeds.

As Mexicans crossed the border into the USA, authorities unfamiliar with cannabis considered the drug capable of giving Mexican's "superhuman strength" and have a "lust for blood".

During this period, Mexicans were likened by Americans to be cockroaches, a metaphor soldiers took and coined the term "roach", the disregarded remains of a used joint.

La cucaracha,
la cucaracha
Ya no puede
caminar
Porque no tiene,
porque le falta
Marihuana que
fumar

The cockroach,
the cockroach
Cannot walk
anymore
Because it hasn't,
because it lacks
Marijuana to
smoke

Pro Tip #4

Before rolling a joint, your cannabis should first be ground down to a fine consistency – think dried oregano – so that the cannabis glows more consistently and with a smoother burn.

Remember Hashish?

Before the weed revolution of recent years – and the increased number of premium quality buds and strains – most of the world had to settle for super-concentrated hashish.

These dried blocks are made by slowly heating and pressing cannabis flowers to create a resin made from the oils contained within.

Once dried, the hashish block can be warmed and then crumbled into a joint with tobacco or smoked in a bong.

While potent, hashish doesn't have the aroma and flavour profiles of Skunk or Chronic.

The Pot Playboy

The Pot Playboy, Jimmy Cournoyer, was the world's largest weed dealer who created a multi-billion-dollar drug-trafficking empire that became associated with pretty much all of America's largest drug cartel, gangs and crime families.

Cournoyer was arrested in 2012 – his disgruntled ex-girlfriend dobbed him in – and he is now serving a 27-year prison sentence. At the peak of his notoriety, Cournoyer was partying with Hollywood A-listers and living a lavish playboy lifestyle.

"Suppose the Russians did something now."

According to *A Very Private Woman: The Life and Unsolved Murder of Presidential Mistress Mary Meyer* by Nina Burleigh (1999), this famous quote was spoken by President John F. Kennedy on the one occasion he allegedly smoked marijuana in the Oval Office to treat his chronic back pain, in July 1962.

It is said that JFK smoked three of six joints brought to him that night by Meyer, his mistress. He refused a fourth joint once the effects of the cannabis kicked in, prompting his immortal line above – a reference to the Cold War with Russia.

Party States

In 2012, Colorado became the first US state to legalize marijuana for recreational use,* with Washington, California and Alaska soon following suit. Colorado now has three times more dispensaries than Starbucks and McDonald's combined!

Today, American states are anything but united when it comes to cannabis, with 26 of the 50 refusing to legalize it... for now.

*California was the first state to legalize medical marijuana in 1996.

US States Where Marijuana is Legal

Alaska, Arizona, California, Colorado, Connecticut, Delaware, Illinois, Maine, Maryland, Massachusetts, Michigan, Minnesota, Missouri, Montana, Nevada, New Jersey, New Mexico, New York, Ohio, Oregon, Rhode Island, Vermont, Virginia, Washington.

Chapter Three

Sweet Leaf

“I think weed is the best drug on earth.”

MILEY CYRUS, *ROLLING STONE*, SEPTEMBER 2013

Weed Playlist #1

1. 'Sweet Leaf' – Black Sabbath
2. 'Legalize It' – Peter Tosh
3. 'Roll Another Number (for the Road)' – Neil Young
4. 'Mary Jane' – Rick James
5. 'Kaya' – Bob Marley
6. 'Pass the Kouchie' – The Mighty Diamonds
7. 'Smoke Two Joints' – The Toyes
8. 'Hits From the Bong' – Cypress Hill
9. 'Because I Got High' – Afroman
10. 'Roll Me Up and Smoke Me When I Die' – Willie Nelson with Snoop Dogg
11. 'Let's Go Get Stoned' – Ray Charles
12. 'Reefer Head Woman' – Aerosmith
13. 'Smoke the Sky' – Motley Crüe

Know Your Smoke

Joint

The first usage of the word joint to mean a hand-rolled "cannabis cigarette" dates back to 1938. But it was in the 1850s that Mexican labourers first used rolling papers to create joints. (Rolling papers were invented in Spain a century before.)

Spliff

The word spliff probably comes from the verb *spiflicate*, a portmanteau of "stifle" and "suffocate". A spliff has a mixture of cannabis and tobacco.

Blunt

For cannabis connoisseurs, blunts take their name from a brand of cigars called Phillies Blunt, which is why blunts are made from hollowed-out cigar wrappers. Cigars are made from rolled tobacco leaf, so effectively they're just fat spliffs.

Toke

A toke is a pull or drag on a joint. It's thought to have derived from the Spanish word *tocar*, meaning "touch", "tap" or "hit", and has been used since the early 1960s.

Icons of Weed #2

Bob Marley

“Herb is natural. Herb is the healin’ of the nation. Everyone on earth is supposed to smoke herb. When you smoke it, we can see and talk real nice and get along. Ya dig it?”

BOB MARLEY,
ANN ARBOR SUN, JUNE 1975

In the early 1970s, Jamaican reggae singer-songwriter Bob Marley's musical fame was equalled by his iconic Rastafarian ideology and herb-smoking. When he died in May 1981, Marley was buried with his favourite bud of marijuana, Lamb's Breath.

In 2014, Bob Marley's estate launched Marley Natural, "the world's first global cannabis brand", according to Cedella Marley, Marley's daughter. The brand sells a multitude of smoking products, including heirloom Jamaican cannabis strains, cannabis-infused lotions and creams, smoking papers and other marijuana-based merchandise.

"My dad would be so happy to see people understanding the healing power of the herb," Cedella told the BBC in November 2014.

Next time you feel giggly and relaxed – and hungry – after smoking a joint, give a high-five to delta-9-tetrahydrocannabinol, or delta-9 THC.

It's the primary active ingredient in cannabis that induces an intoxicating, psychoactive effect.

The cannabinoid was first isolated by Dr Raphael Mechoulam at the University of Tel Aviv in 1964.

$C_{21}H_{30}O_2$

The chemical formula for tetrahydrocannabinol, or THC, the psychoactive compound found in cannabis.

“I was a fugitive for six and a half years and I smuggled as much cannabis as I could.”

HOWARD MARKS, *MR NICE*, 1996

Mr Nice

The world's most-loved cannabis smuggler was the charming Welshman, Howard Marks, AKA Mr Nice. At the peak of his power in the 1980s, Marks was the boss of a multi-million-dollar drug-smuggling empire, with a personal net worth of more than £48 million ($63 million).

In December 1979, Marks smuggled the largest ever shipment of cannabis, from Colombia to the UK – 50 tons (45 tonnes) – enough to make Britain happy for a whole year. Marks was able to ship huge volume by devising an ingenious strategy: he used the sound equipment of British rock bands (not always real) to smuggle cannabis through the USA.

In 1988, he was given a 25-year prison sentence, of which he served seven years. After his release, Marks penned his autobiography, *Mr Nice* (1996). It became an international bestseller and is thoroughly recommended.

Sex, Drugs & Rock'n'Roll

After several decades having its reputation dragged through the mud as "the Devil's Herb", cannabis made a comeback with the countercultural movement in the early 1960s, when artists such as Bob Dylan, the Beatles and the Rolling Stones were seen publicly smoking weed.

It is often agreed that cannabis' arrival into the larger cultural conscience came at 1969's Woodstock Festival, New York, where it was reported that 99 per cent of its 500,000 attendees openly smoked weed. Many of the festival's headliners – the Who, Santana, Jimi Hendrix and Grateful Dead – were prominent, and proud, weed promotors too.

“I’d been a rather straight working-class lad but when we started to get into pot it seemed to me to be quite uplifting. It didn’t seem to have too many side effects like alcohol or pills, which I pretty much kept off. I liked marijuana. I didn’t have a hard time with it and to me it was mind-expanding.”

PAUL MCCARTNEY, *PAUL MCCARTNEY: MANY YEARS FROM NOW*, 1997

Just a Herb

The Hispanic term for cannabis – *marijuana* – is most commonly used in the Americas. It is believed the word comes from the Spanish *mejorana*, or marjoram, a species of perennial herb similar to oregano.

Marijuana became a popular name for cannabis in the USA around the 1850s, when Mexicans freely crossed the borders bringing weed with them.

Reefer Madness

In 1936, weed stock took a heavy blow. The release of the Hollywood movie, *Reefer Madness*, directed by Louis J. Gasnier, was intended to scare parents and teenagers about the dangers of cannabis culture.

The plot is both hilarious and disturbing: high school students are lured by dealers to smoke weed. When they do, they become addicted – and go on to commit violent crimes, such as a hit-and-run, murder and attempted rape.

Reefer Madness is now regarded as one of the worst films ever made, though admittedly it's a great film to watch when having a smoke. Oh, the irony.

Top Producers

Today, cannabis is big business. In America, there are more than 13,000 active and legal cannabis farms.

The top five growing states are Colorado, California, Michigan, Washington and Oregon, which are growing more than 2,750 tons (2,500 metric tonnes) a year combined.

Classic of the Materia Medica, a pharmacopeia attributed to the mythical Chinese Emperor Shennong, was the first written record to list cannabis as a medicine – compiled more than 2,000 years ago – during the Han Dynasty.

Regarded as the father of Chinese medicine, Shennong's botanical manual also introduced the health benefits of acupuncture, and more than 350 herbal medicines for the first time, including ginseng.

“I’m kind of the canary in the mine, if people are wondering what happens if you smoke that shit a long time.”

WILLIE NELSON, *ROLLING STONE*, APRIL 2019

Icons of Weed #3

Willie Nelson

According to *Rolling Stone* (April 2019), Willie Nelson is "America's most legendary stoner and a walking testament to weed".

For more than seven decades, Nelson, now in his nineties, has been a weed smoker and a powerful advocate of its decriminalization for most of his adult life. A famed country singer who has released more than 100 albums, Nelson is an ideal role model for the positive health benefits of cannabis.

"I think people need to be educated to the fact that marijuana is not a drug," Nelson told the *Texas Observer* (August 2015). "Marijuana is an herb and a flower. God put it here. If He put it here and He wants it to grow, what gives the government the right to say that God is wrong?"

300 Acres

The largest single bust of cannabis at a cannabis farm came in 2011, in a remote desert area of Baja, California, when US authorities discovered a cannabis plantation that consisted of 300 acres (120 hectares) of land growing many tens of thousands marijuana plants, many of which were more than 8 feet (2.5 metres) tall. Police destroyed the crops immediately but not before adding up its street value: $160 million (£120 million).

The legal cannabis industry is now larger than the worldwide tobacco industry.

Global sales of medical and adult-use cannabis and CBD hit $45 billion (£34.4 billion) in 2024. The market is expected to double in two years to reach a value of over $101 billion (£77 billion) by 2026.

Pro Tip #5

There's no such thing as a perfect joint – all joints are created equal.

Having said that, the best ratio of weed to paper is:

½ gram of weed to a single rolling paper (1¼ in/3 cm wide).

If you use larger papers, use more weed.

Queen's Orders

In 1563, Queen Elizabeth I ordered landowners with 60 acres (24 hectares) or more to grow cannabis or face a £5 fine, around £1,200 ($1,500) today. Not to smoke, of course, but to grow for hemp, a vital component of rope to be used for Britain's rapidly expanding seafaring empire.

However, Elizabeth is not the only royal to have procured cannabis. Prince Harry has too. He admitted to smoking weed regularly in his 2023 autobiography, *Spare*. "Marijuana really did help me," he wrote. No other modern royals have admitted to smoking weed.

While the leaves of a cannabis plant are iconic, you don't generally smoke them. In the main, only the buds, or flowers, are smoked.

Each cannabis leaf is known as a "palmate compound leaf", which on average has seven leaflets, each one with its famous serrated edges that help the cannabis plant cope in cold weather.

Stoned or High?

For decades, the two main phrases related to feeling the psychoactive effects of cannabis ("getting stoned" and "getting high") are used interchangeably and paradoxically mean the same thing, yet are complete opposites.

The term "stoned", could have come from the feeling of being knocked down by stones (or feeling as heavy as a stone), brought on by the indica strain's perceived mood-relaxing vibe; or perhaps evolved from the Italian *stonato* to mean "dazed and confused".

The term "high" could originate from the sativa strain's perceived mood-elevating vibe.

5 December 1484

On this day, Roman Pope Innocent VIII – born Giovanni Battista Cybo – issued a papal ban on cannabis medicines calling them "unholy sacrament of the satanic mass", or as we call it today, "the Devil's cabbage".

The pope believed cannabis was used by witches and devil-worshippers for witchcraft – superstitions that were prevalent in late medieval Europe.

In the same papal decree he called for the execution of all black cats too.

Since 1200 BCE, Hindus have been consuming *bhang* – dried cannabis leaves, seeds and stems – every year during their spring festivals of Maha Shivratri and Holi.

The leaves of the cannabis plant are smashed and dried, and either eaten whole or mixed with milk and drunk. The high takes about three hours to kick in.

Bhang is mentioned in the Hindu sacred text *Atharva Veda* and referred to as "sacred grass".

An Experiment

On 10 December 2013, Uruguay became the world's first nation to legalize the cultivation, sale and possession of cannabis and the first country to implement a state-run marijuana marketplace. Today, citizens are even allowed to cultivate up to six plants at home.

However, just because it was made legal, President Tabaré Vázquez, who oversaw the legalization during his leadership tenure, did not recommend its usage, calling it an "experiment".

In a live national TV address (covered by the *Guardian*, December 2014), Vázquez's opening statement was: "First of all, you shouldn't consume drugs."

The Munchies

If you've wanted to know why smoking weed gives you the insatiable desire to eat snacks – known as "the munchies" – blame your endocannabinoid system, the complex area of your brain that regulates mood, sleep, appetite, memory and energy.

Research shows that when THC is ingested into a smoker's body it interacts with cannabinoid receptors in the brain that regulate emotions, pain and our sense of smell and taste, and enhances our sensitivity to both, which in turn releases a hormone, called ghrelin, which stimulates hunger. Now you know.

Chapter Four

The High Life

Cannabidiol (CBD)

It was in 1940 that American chemist Roger Adams discovered that a *Cannabis sativa* plant contained two key ingredients – Tetrahydrocannabinol (THC) and Cannabidiol (CBD).

Adams was the first to isolate CBD from a cannabis plant, and hypothesize about the existence of Tetrahydrocannabinol. THC was later isolated in 1964, and has now been studied comprehensively, allowing for purer, more potent strains to be cultivated.

CBD today is found in thousands of products that are promoted to treat chronic pain, anxiety, inflammation and insomnia.

Pro Tip #6

When too much THC has been absorbed into the body, users can experience a discomforting sensation known as a "whitey". (Don't worry, we've all been there.)

Symptoms can manifest in different ways but usually users turn pale, then do a combination of fainting, vomiting, sweating, going dizzy, getting The Fear and suffering intense anxiety. The body does this because of cannabis' anticholinergic effects: it inhibits nerve impulses responsible for various bodily functions, causing the user's senses to plummet.

If you "pull a whitey", don't panic. Simply rehydrate slowly and often, breathe deeply and regulate your blood sugar levels by drinking fresh juice or eating a low-carb snack. You'll be back to normal in no time.

Medical Marijuana

In the last two decades, much has been written about scientific studies by medical specialists concerning the positive health benefits of ingesting marijuana for medicinal purposes.

Put simply, cannabis is recommended by some physicians to help alleviate symptoms of depression, post-traumatic stress disorder, social anxiety, chronic pain, epilepsy, multiple sclerosis, nausea and vomiting caused by chemotherapy, to name a few.

However, there are negative side effects of ingesting cannabis regularly too, according to the US Department of Justice, so do your research.

A Costly Spliff

Remember the moment in 2018 when the world's richest man, Elon Musk, smoked a spliff (a mixture of weed with tobacco) on the *Joe Rogan Experience*, the planet's most popular podcast? "I'm not a regular smoker of weed," he told Rogan.

Musk made headline news around the world, and in the aftermath, the share prices of his electric vehicle company, Tesla, plunged by 10 per cent – more than $20 billion (£15 billion) (according to NBC News, 2018). As a result of this harmless smoke, Musk also had to appease shareholders and be drug-tested for a whole year.

Proposition 215

In November 1996, California became the first US state to approve the posession of cannabis – if used for a medical condition. This law was known as Proposition 215.

Anyone caught with "medical marijuana" by police would be exempt from criminal liability. This was the first domino to fall in America's loosening of cannabis laws.

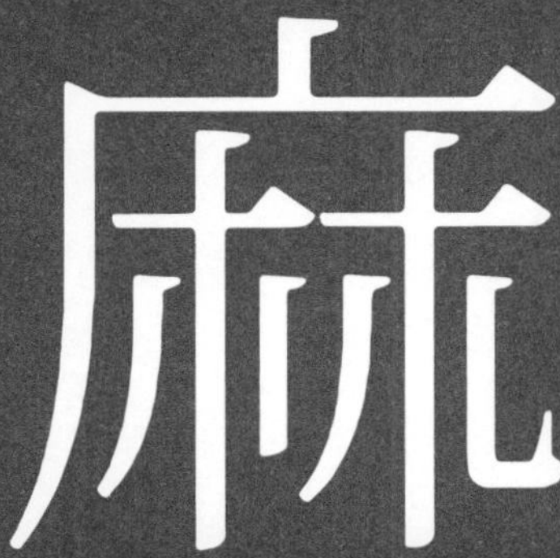

In China, cannabis is known as *má*, the oldest recorded name for cannabis. The character for má depicts two plants under a shelter. Interestingly, the same character also means "numbness".

The use of cannabis as a medicine in western China dates back 4,800 years.

"Drugs are everywhere in our society. They are omniscient. If you look at the amount of pot that was smoked in the United States last year, that would reach the moon."

MICHAEL SCOTT, *THE OFFICE*, 'DRUG TESTING', 2006

Space Cakes

You don't have to light a joint to get high. Weed brownies, or space cakes, are a delicious way to get a buzz without the smoke. Before gummies, space cakes were the first edible.

To make a space cake, simply prepare your usual brownie recipe, but as you melt the butter sprinkle in a small amount – ⅓ oz (9 g) should do to feed a group – of finely ground weed. The cannabis will dissolve in the butter's fat.

Remember: the effects of a space cake take a lot longer to kick in than smoking a joint. Wait at least 90 minutes before eating any more.

Once you munch, you cannot go back!

You Know You're High When...

1. You say, "I gotta write this down!", after thinking something "profound".
2. Ten minutes feels like an hour, but an hour feels like ten minutes.
3. Your joints get increasingly soggier throughout the night.
4. You say, "I can't deal with this", when somebody says something too serious.
5. You find particular words exceptionally difficult to say.
6. You find a specific person the most hilarious and have no idea why.
7. You think to yourself, "Do I seem weird? Why is everyone else totally fine?"
8. You attempt to make a super-joint using 37 rolling papers. (You never finish it.)
9. Everything tastes delicious even though your mouth is as dry as sand.
10. You run out of rolling papers.

The first person ever to be arrested for possession of weed in the USA was 23-year-old African American Moses Baca – one day after the Marihuana Tax Act 1937 came into effect.

The arrest occurred in Denver, Colorado, when police allegedly found ¼ ounce (7 grams) of weed in his house. He served 18 months in a Kansas prison.

“Shit, man, I’m gonna be late for work again. That’s the fifth time this week, and it’s only Tuesday, man.”

CHEECH MARIN, *CHEECH & CHONG’S NEXT MOVIE*, 1980

Cheech & Chong

Cheech Marin and Tommy Chong are the undisputed kings of stoner comedies. Their 1978 cult classic *Up in Smoke* is perhaps the finest work in the genre – it's beyond hilarious – and is effectively the two comedians getting high and causing chaos. Try these too...

1. *Cheech & Chong's Next Movie* (1980)
2. *Nice Dreams* (1981)
3. *Things Are Tough All Over* (1982)
4. *Still Smokin'* (1983)
5. *Cheech & Chong's The Corsican Brothers* (1984)
6. *Get Out of My Room* (1985)
7. *Cheech & Chong's Animated Movie!* (2013)

What Do You Call It?

Everyone knows dope, Ganja, marijuana, weed, pot and grass. But, according to *Time*'s comprehensive research in 2017, there are more than 1,200 other slang words for cannabis known to the US Drug Enforcement Agency that (presumably) has to keep a record of these things. Many of these terms date back to the jazz era of the 1920s and '30s when marijuana was popular among the American underground. Here are some of our favourites...

1. Jazz Cabbage
2. Devil's Lettuce
3. Reefer
4. Doobie
5. Mary Jane
6. Purple Haze
7. Sticky Icky
8. Zaza
9. Maui Wowie
10. KGB
11. Green Goddess
12. Holy Weed
13. Houdini
14. Grass
15. Jive
16. Broccoli
17. Catnip

“We were smoking marijuana for breakfast.”

JOHN LENNON, AS QUOTED IN
THE BEATLES ANTHOLOGY, 1970

“The Scythians take some of this hemp-seed and, creeping under the felt coverings, throw it upon the red-hot stones; immediately it smokes, and gives out such a vapour as no Grecian vapour-bath can exceed; the Scyths, delighted, shout for joy.”

HERODOTUS, *THE HISTORY OF HERODOTUS*, C.440 BCE

Cannabis

The word "cannabis" comes from a group of nomadic peoples known as the Scythians, originating from the country we now know as Iran.

While the Chinese were the first to employ cannabis for its medicinal qualities, it was the Scythians who first taught the world to get high and used cannabis for its psychoactive effects.

According to contemporary historian Herodotus, ancient Greeks observed Scythian funeral rituals as they burned cannabis flowers to inhale the vapours and induce a trance-like state.

Cannabis Beer – Oh Yes!

Studies in the last decade have proven that *Humulus lupulus* (the plant that makes hops, the active flavour ingredient in beer) and *Cannabis sativa* are genetically close within the Cannabaceae plant family. The only difference is that hops lack an enzyme to convert cannabigerolic acid into THC. However, with genetic engineering, this has been achieved.

And so, may we introduce... the world's first cannabis beer.

This isn't just beer laced with marijuana. This is beer brewed using the actual stalk, stem and roots of cannabis plants. Created by Canadian scientists in 2019, and containing 6.5 milligrams of THC per beer, Province Brands promise the cannabis beer "hits you very quickly, which is not common for a marijuana edible", and tastes "dry, savoury and less sweet than a typical beer".

Dabbing

The latest evolution of weed smoking has arrived! Named after the hip-hop dance (in which one arm is bent at an angle across the chest while the other is fully extended parallel to the first arm, with the face turned toward the bent elbow), dabbing is the process of inhaling concentrated THC using an electronic cigarette – what the kids call a vape.

Smoking and vaping THC-rich extracts from the marijuana plant (a practice called dabbing) is on the rise.

The Biggest Brownie

In 2021, a Massachusetts-based cannabis company MariMed Inc. celebrated National Brownie Day – 8 December – by making the world's largest edible brownie, according to Guinness World Records. It's a monster. Google it.

It contained a staggering 20,000 milligrams of THC as well as: 1,344 eggs, 250 pounds of sugar, 212 pounds of butter, 5 pounds of vanilla extract, 81 pounds of flour, 2 pounds of baking powder, 3 pounds of salt and 122 pounds of cocoa powder.

After baking, it weighed over 60 stone (385 kg) and measured 3 x 3 feet (nearly 1 x 1 metres).

Weed Around the World

Just in case you need it on your travels, here's a list of the good stuff in some other languages...

1. *Bhang/Ganja* – Hindi
2. *Cáñamo* – Spanish
3. *Canapa* – Italian
4. *Cần sa* – Vietnamese
5. *Chanvre* – French
6. *Hanf* – German
7. *Hampa* – Swedish
8. *Hashish* – Arabic
9. *Hennep* – Dutch
10. *Kạychā* – Thai
11. *Kenevir* – Turkish
12. *Konope* – Polish
13. *Maconha* – Portuguese
14. *Pakalolo* – Hawaiian

Female of the Species

The most-grown strain of *Cannabis sativa* is sinsemilla as it has a particularly high concentration of THC, the psychoactive chemicals responsible for getting high.

Only female cannabis plants, like sinsemilla, can produce potent high THC buds. Male plants do not produce any buds at all – their main duty is to simply pollinate the female plants by dispersing pollen. (Cannabis is anemophilous – pollinated by wind. Cannabis plants rely on wind to transfer pollen from male to female plants.)

Like most things in nature, it is the female of the species that is the boss.

Icons of Weed #4

Irvin Rosenfeld

Irvin Rosenfeld is an icon for stoners. In 2014, Guinness World Records verified his claim to be the world's "most prolific weed smoker".

For 40 years, Rosenfeld smoked ten medical joints a day (that's more than 120,000 in total!) to ease the chronic and painful conditions surrounding his rare bone tumour disorder. During that time, Rosenfeld was one of just four patients who legally received weed from the US government.

World's Longest Joint

The world's longest joint – to date, at least – was created in 2017 at the Harvest Cup, Massachusetts, by a group of dedicated weed enthusiasts.

The joint reached 100 feet (30 metres) in length and required 5 pounds (2.3 kilograms) of cannabis to fill it. It was certified as the longest joint in the world, though not by Guinness World Records, as it was considered an illegal activity.

It took its creators *four hours* to smoke.

“If everyone smoked weed, the world would be a better place.”

KIRSTEN DUNST, *LIVE* MAGAZINE, 2007

Types of Joint

Aside from the standard cigarette-style cone-shape, joints can come in scores of shapes and sizes. These are the most common...

1. The Dutch Tulip – long and thin, then fat and thick, like a tulip!
2. Cross Joint – shaped like a cross
3. The Shotgun – two joints wrapped together in paper, smoked side by side
4. The Plumber – normal joint, but with a tunnel in the centre (use a wooden stick)
5. The Windmill – four joints joined, in a windmill-shape, to a fat central one

$24K

According to *Forbes*, the most expensive joint ever rolled contained 1.5 pounds (770 g) of premium weed and measured 30 inches (76 cm) long. It was auctioned at a value of $24,000 (£18,000)!

The joint also contained 24-carat gold rolling papers to boot. The lucky buyer purchased the joint to celebrate California's legalization of recreational marijuana in 2012. Who's got a light?

“The weed doesn’t take away; it’s an attribute, an accolade.”

SNOOP DOGG, *OBSERVER*, APRIL 2015